maybe she's born with it, maybe it's **TRAUMA**

Poems

CAIT THOMSON

Beyond The Veil Press

Created on the lands of the Ute, Arapahoe, and Cheyenne peoples, in the so-called United States of America.

ISBN: 9798387206788

TABLE OF CONTENTS

INTRODUCTION

Maybe She's Born With It, Maybe It's Trauma! is the title of Cait Thomson's new collection of poems. While I'm not prepared to clear up that question, after reading this gutsy book, I am prepared to assert that Thomson is a funny, courageous, gifted writer, willing not only to face her demons, but to tickle them and to tweak their noses.

"moderation is not in my vocabulary" Thomson states in *i ate watermelon until i made myself sick* (Thomson has a way with titles). One has no trouble believing it after learning Thomson compulsively brushed her cat "*until she had a bald spot.*" This piece mostly consists of deft self-analysis, delivered in a punchy, staccato style. Then, in a perfect example of the humor one encounters throughout the book, she closes the piece: "*it is also possible/that she was an old cat/and losing her hair."*

You'll notice in the above quotations, lowercase letters appear where convention calls for uppercase. I am a formalist, and usually such deviations would rankle. In this case, however, Thomson has made a wise decision. There is a modesty and reserve here that is inherently lowercase. As Thomson puts it in *double depresso to go* (my favorite piece in the collection, a masterpiece of timorousness, if that's not an oxymoron): ". . .*all comes back to this:my/heart is very small, i am/. . . so tired.*"

It's impossible not to draw strength from Thomson's moxie, or not to be amused by her strategies for dealing with this messy thing called life. There's chutzpah here and heart. Trauma be damned!

-Peter Whisenant, writer

TRIGGER WARNING

This chapbook contains works dealing with or making mention to anxiety, depression, suicidal ideation, childhood trauma, and sexual assault.

Please take care of yourself as you read through these intimate experiences and reach out for help if you need it.

We love you. Thank you for reading.

United States
Suicide and Mental Health Crisis Line: 988
Suicide Prevention Line: 1.800.273.8255
Sexual Assault Hotline: 1.800.656.4673
Domestic Violence Hotline: 1.800.799.7233
Substance Abuse Hotline: 1.800.662.4357
Self-Harm Textline: Text "Connect" to 741741

Canada
Talk Suicide Canada: 1-833-456-4566
Quebec residents: 1-866-277-3553 or visit *suicide.ca*
Wellness Together: 1-866-585-0445 or text WELLNESS to 741741
Hope For Wellness (First Peoples, Inuit, and Métis Peoples):
1-855-242-3310 or connect to online chat: *hopeforwellness.ca*

United Kingdom
Samaritans 116 123

Australia
Lifeline Australia 13 11 14
Beyond Blue 1300 22 4636

Please reach out if there's a resource we can add here.
More resources at the back of this book and on our website: beyondtheveilpress.com.

maybe she's born with it, maybe it's TRAUMA

Poems

CAIT THOMSON

Beyond The Veil Press

to the group chat
long may it reign

sunday, january 1

to do list

- make doctor appointment
- make dentist appointment
- make optometry appointment
- make gynecologist appointment
- oh and a therapy appointment
- take pills
- brush my teeth
- brush her teeth
- floss her teeth too
- can anyone tell i'm not flossing?
- should we be brushing the cats' teeth?

  Google: should i brush my cats teeth?
  Google: what does cat gingivitis look like?
- Make vet appointments for all four cats
- go for a walk
- do some yoga
- meal planning for the week

  Google: recipes for picky kids
  Google: how much iron does a 5 year old need?
  Google: signs of iron deficiency in kids
  Google: foods with high iron content
  Google: foods with high iron content that kids will eat
- buy apples
- fold laundry
- fill the bird feeders
- clean cat litter
- pick up cat food
- remember to ask vet about olive's weight

  Google: how to help a cat lose weight?
  Google: how to tell if a cat is depressed?
  Google: how to cheer up a cat?
- clean sleep machine, it's been way too long
- shop for birthday party decorations

- research gymnastic classes

  Google: is gymnastics safe for little girls?
  Google: "ottawa" and "gymnastics coach" and "sexual assault"
  Google: kids soccer leagues near me
- return books to the library
- respond to emails and messages
- make time for   myself?

it feels like i'm running out of time

monday, january 2

the lies we tell

i'm fine, thanks, and you?
by which i mean i'm good

by which i mean i'm doing ok

by which i mean i'm surviving, not thriving lol

by which i mean i'm having a hard time

by which i mean i'm struggling
struggling with being present right now

by which i mean it is a monumental task
to get out of bed

by which i mean i think about brushing my teeth
getting some fresh air
calling up a friend
and then decide why bother

by which i mean i'm so tired i could sleep for a thousand years
but instead i scroll through the entirety of instagram at 2 am
in this forever pandemic that has become an average day

by which i mean this never-ending anxiety
this forever pandemic
this emotional binging that never comes close to filling me
this darkness that always comes when i shut my eyes

is killing me

by which i mean i'm fine, thanks
and you?

tuesday, january 3

maybe she's born with it, maybe it's trauma!*

what is her secret, you ask?
she has that ~new therapist~ glow!
puffy eyes, snot stained cheeks!
the signature blotchy, red face
that comes from walking yet another stranger
through your childhood for 50 minutes!
the look is elevated by the glossy lips
that are all the rage this season!
the shine comes from the post-session
quarter pounder with cheese!
you too can achieve this look
for only $180 an hour!**
what a steal!

**or attention-deficit/hyperactivity disorder or autism or borderline personality disorder or bipolar disorder or what is the point of a diagnosis anyways you aren't broken you don't need to be fixed*

***price does not include any additional socio-economic, physiological, or other costs that inevitably come with trauma recovery and the treatment of mental illness*

wednesday, january 4

i hyperventilate in my sleep

i don't remember my dreams
but my body does

i don't tell you this for the sympathy
but so you can try to understand
there are whole multitudes of people
eyes bright with childlike wonderterror
eyes bright because there's no oxygen

i don't tell you this for the sympathy
but so you can try to understand
i don't want to be fixed anymore
some things there's just no fixing
some things there's just no outrunning

but if you could just stay with me
while i try to catch my breath

i'm sorry

it's easier for everyone
when i write about love

ah but isn't this
just another one about love

thursday, january 5

i ate watermelon until i made myself sick

and then i brushed our cat
until she had a bald spot.

i imagine this says something about me.

maybe i care too much.
i try too hard.
i give too easily.
i overthink and under deliver.

i cared
and i tried
and i gave
until that poor cat
felt the breeze on her naked skin
for the first time in her life.

moderation is not in my vocabulary
and it has ~~never~~ always been a problem.

and now there's too much of me.
i am just too much of everything.
i am a wrecking ball.
i am a destroyer of worlds.
i am excess embodied.
i am overwhelming and overwhelmed.

it is also possible
that she was an old cat
and losing her hair.

friday, january 6

fri·day·night
/ˈfrīˌdā nīt,ˈfrīdē nīt/ (after rudy francisco)

noun

1. the evening of the day before saturday and following thursday
2. the brief moment in time when she laughs with her friend the moon, forgets all of her responsibilities except breathing, watches a cult classic action movie from the 1980's and becomes like the hungry hungry caterpillar by consuming: one bowl of farm boy brand russet potato salt and vinegar chips; one bag of haribo gummy bears; one nanaimo bar; one gin and tonic; another bowl of chips; one glass of milk; one more nanaimo bar; and lastly, one good man.

russet potato chips will change your life
trust me

saturday, january 7

"IS JEAN CLAUDE VAN DAMME REALLY A SPY"

i left myself this
note late on a friday night
i demand answers

i'm unhinged
i'm untethered
i'm liable to float away like a balloon
only to explode like the hindenberg
you wouldn't want to miss that

sunday, january 8

lately i've been feeling very uninspired and overwhelmed giving one hundred percent to family friends the nine to five job leaves no energy for creativity and creativity is what makes it all seem worthwhile but it's no fun either when it feels like i'm letting down my family friends the nine to five job and i'm not sure if i'll ever get to be who or what i want and how is that not completely soul crushing to everyone else and i keep saying i just need a break but how does one week off work solve the sourness in my gut i don't want to have to work to live but i know poetry will never pay the bills and it feels like we're on the cusp of something big but i think it will be too late for me and it feels like all i do is complain when really i'm just grateful to be here for another day

you know?

you know?

lately i've been feeling like
a will-o'-wisp
a gender reveal
gone wrong
pink and blue smoke
turning to grey
just to muddy the waters
a ghost
in a nightgown
hovering
at the top of the stairs
i have two young girls
calling to me in the night

monday, january 9

anxiety attack in d minor

some days are harder than others
and today feels crushing
like heart breaking
like lungs bursting
like i can't keep living like this
but there is no relief
like everyone i know sees a therapist
but i feel like i'm the only one going crazy
like i'm afraid this is all there is
and i'm afraid that it's not enough
like i'm tired of my body
feeling like someone else's home
like i am wasting my life
being afraid of dying
being afraid of living
when do i breathe
when do i breathe
when is it my turn to breathe
icantbreatheicantbreatheicantbreatheicantbreatheicantbreatheicantbreathe
i think my heart will explode
this is so stupid
sostupidsostupidsostupidsostupidsostupidsostupidsostupidsostupidsostupid
i can't keep living like this
i can't keep living

like this

i can't

tuesday, january 10

five daily non-negotiables
(excerpt from therapy homework)

1. pet a cat (or two or three or four)
2. drink enough water
3. get some fresh air
4. do something that i enjoy
5. let go of the guilt

how can this have happened?
i've forgotten how to live

wednesday, january 11

double depresso to go

i am so tired, my heart is
very small. life has torn

away at it and there is
always a new ache to join

the others. look, this new
one is a hangnail. what i

mean to say is this ache
catches on everything. i

want to write pages and
pages about this but it

all comes back to this: my
heart is very small, i am

so tired.

i didn't take very good care of myself today
tomorrow is another chance to prove to myself
i'm worth the effort

this shouldn't be so hard

thursday, january 12

times are hard but poetry works harder

you see, i had given up
on a lot of things
(almost poetry too)
and then i heard the news

a friend, jules, has written a book
beautiful things are happening to good people!
also
good things are happening to beautiful people!

it makes me feel good and beautiful too

i have a hard time
feeling good and beautiful
for any length of time at all

friday, january 13

feels

it feels like i'll never get better
it feels like i'll always be this way
it feels like wow! i should be kinder to myself
but how! how do people do it!
it feels like fuck! its not my fault i'm this way
but fuck! i'm the only one that can fix it
but i'm tired

please could i get a day off
please could i tap someone in
if my mind is wrestling match
i could really use a friend with a folding chair
but inner child, please, have some patience
the only way to make it to ~~forty~~ carnegie hall
is practice, baby

so it's a bad day
i'm not weak or stupid or unworthy of love
i'm funny and caring and creative
i'm healing and its hard and that's ok for today

practice, baby, practice

saturday, january 14

overthinking again

i am obsessed with meaningless riddles
after all, they provide ample distraction
from the meaningful ones

for example!
is it worthwhile to get fake nails
they make me feel good
but $70 good?

truthfully
they don't have to cost me $70
they wouldn't if i didn't tip 30%
but i'm too much a burden
sewn together by catgut guilt

here's another good riddle!
if the stars
we see bright in the sky
have already exploded and died
does someone
across the infinity of space
see our sun and wonder
how long has it been since it exploded

and why does that make me feel
afraid

sunday, january 15

some girls, april 2000
(after kayla czaga)

some girls were anxious
some girls were always sick to their stomach
couldn't keep down food
such a mystery

some girls were adopted by other girls
and given make-overs
ripped inside out and called much better

some girls looked for attention
to dress up as affection
age/sex/location lies through their teeth

some girls spat wasps
and blood
and apologies
other girls ate poison to feel something new

some girls told other girls late at night
that swallowing is love
some girls swallowed fear for every meal
isn't that love

some girls thought love was a cheek
bit through in the night

some girls hid in the back woods
in the dark
in the closet
and held their breath
waiting to be ~~found~~ saved

some girls sweat through white blouses
and called it a school dance

some girls skipped church and school
better to bleed at home instead

monday, january 16

the rodent control aisle of canadian tire

last night was snowy and cold
and we could hear mice in the floor again
it was comforting in a way
the quiet gnawing
the gentle scrabbling
their return predicting the deep freeze
an entire world that goes on without us

i wonder if the mother gets tired
of feeding her children bird seed
taken from a chewed hole in the bag
i wonder if she gets tired of the dark
tired of the lingering smell of compost
tired of losing babies to the cold
or to her own hunger

i wonder why she chose
this house to make her home
maybe because she sensed hearts
our gentle hearts

we stood in the rodent control aisle of canadian tire
and threw our hands up in frustration

we bought another bag of bird seed instead

tuesday, january 17

there's a golden girl in my stomach

my therapist has asked me
to practice listening to my gut
so once a day i crouch down
and try to give her my full attention

some people call it their inner child
me, i have a golden girl in my stomach
she has the voice of bea arthur
with the attitude of dorothy zbornak

listen she says
you deserve the respect and love
you show to everyone else
now show it to yourself
you putz

or the other day she told me
no one cares what you look like
but they can smell you in space
have a shower sweetheart

just now i can hear her muttering
ten dollars for a head of romaine?
what are they smoking?
oh and by the way
you're doing a great job honey
i'm proud of you

wednesday, january 18

the closest i've ever been to being me

it occurs to me that not everyone
is on a journey of life or death self discovery
some people wake up and know who they are
i hope those ~~assholes~~ lucky ducks appreciate their good fortune

me, i feel like national treasure nic cage
and i'm this close to the declaration of independence
fingertips dancing along the glass
i've assumed that weird nic cage face: eyebrow cocked, mouth pursed

i feel like i'm the closest to understanding myself
that i've ever been
and when i finally get there
to a place where everything makes sense

i know i'll be con air nic cage
and won't that be amazing
i mean, he's never been sexier
and the hair! wow! and what a happy ending!

except for las vegas of course
but the city's had a good run

ok
ok
ok
buscemi has me worried too

thursday, january 19

captain's log, stardate 41153.7.
(blackout of picard's captain's log from star trek: the next generation, episode 1)

friday, january 20

monster train

how are your intrusive thoughts?
mine arrive like an express train

if my mind is supple and well-rested
the train quickly pulls out of the station
i barely have time to glimpse
what is scratching at the windows

but other times
the train makes an unplanned stop
panic
screeching spidery trails
the glass can only hold for so long
maybe if i close my eyes and pray
maybe if i sit on my hands
maybe if i tell someone
steady now
shattering shattering shattering
oh shit
here they come

if poets are the canaries
this mine is about to blow

saturday, january 21

night

1.
there is a man running laps
in a pitch black field
you can just see his breath
confident white clouds
i quickly march back to the car
in the pitch black lot
keys between knuckles
anxious silver talons

2.
it's 4 am
i'm out looking for children's tylenol again
there is frost and my breathe floats away
as if it has somewhere better to be
the stars are so bright i can practically hear them
a million microscopic crystal bells
the stars are so bright but they cant compete
with the costco parking lot
insignificant and obscene and oh the cheek of it
i think we've done this all wrong

3.
when i lay my head down at night
all i can hear is
"how are you doing -
when
are you
coming back
to workworkworkworkworkworkworkworkworkworkworkworkworkwork

sunday, january 22

blackberries make me nervous

like russian roulette gun to my head anxiety
things can look innocent at first glance
tiny glossy cushions of purple twilight
just begging to be burst across a tongue

i've had enough blackberries to know
bitterness lurks
yucky mold taste lingers
like that time i ate a white chocolate truffle
that was supposed to be kept refrigerated
and for one brief moment i thought
"wow! blue cheese flavour! bold!"
but it was actually passion fruit filling
way way way past its best before date

when you're luckyfoolhardybrave enough
to bite into the kind of blackberry
you thought only existed in fairytales
savour it

you idiot
savour it

monday, january 23

this is a poem about a bird
(after julie stenton)

it was a red breasted nuthatch
that watched me from the side

of a white cedar. i filled my palm
with sunflower seeds and held my

breath. he hopped down the tree
trunk to silently flit onto my out-

stretched fingers. and this tiny bird
couldn't weight more than 10 grams

but somehow when he took flight
again, he carried the entire heaviness

of my heart effortlessly away between
his delicate feet.

poetry is the symptom and the cure
the wound and the balm
around and around i go

tuesday, january 24

for brian

isn't it funny
life got so easy
once i let you love me
once i let myself believe someone could love me
like you do

me:
made solely from
mental illness
and memory foam

you once asked for a poem
well, here goes:

roses are red
her irises are blue
there is no poetry
in my life without you

wednesday, january 25

i'm not sure i understand existentialism

it turns
out this life has
no meaning which somehow
makes everything more meaningful
all these
turns around the sun knowing you
no thanks to god or fate
therein lies the
magic

thursday, january 26

saltwater

some days i am the oyster
some days i am the grain of sand
some days i am even the pearl

and some days i am the blue infinite ocean
more vast than my body my worries or what i make of them

friday, january 27

thoughts for mina: 2023 ad

mina i'm buzzing
a sound wants to escape from my mouth
- like a bird
an explosion of feathers
i've flown too close to the sun

mina
fowl fireworks
poprocks
stars between my teeth
look! what flavour is this one
blood red cherry

hungry
not for kneeling
but for something that's never been seen
just a rumour from the upside down
where winter is summer
and our parents walk in the clouds

mina
imagine feeling construction vest safety
bold bright almost hurts the eyes to see it
imagine wearing that love
whenever you left the house
mina it's real

mina
don't give in to despair
hop on my shoulders
let's pick this life clean of apples
crisp tender flesh
let's wrap everything in pastry
and call it a day

saturday, january 28

every night before bed

i kiss the cats goodnight
good night i love you
good night i love you
good night i love you
good night i love you
every night before bed
i kiss my daughter goodnight
good night i love you
every night before bed
i kiss my husband goodnight
good night i love you
every night before bed
i marvel at how a broken heart
can still be so full

sunday, january 29

intermission in feeling better

it feels like i'm failing
it feels like i'm flailing
it feels like i'm a bird
with one wing
its hard not to imagine
things would be easier –
ah nevermind
my doctor says this
kind of thinking is
called passive suicidal ideation
and that healing is not
a straight line
and neither am i
i am the squirrel
eating from the
eggnog carton feeder
the one filled with
bird seed and old bacon fat
she is desperate
but she is determined
to survive
the winter

my therapist says i spend too much time
looking at my own brain

monday, january 30

ursus maritimus

my cat, chicken, has a lot of white spots.
depending on the light, she can be pure

as snow or creamy yellow like a polar
bear. i was raised by polar bears so i

know how dangerous they can be. she
has been patient with me for shrinking

when she shows her pointed teeth. i am
learning that we all have the potential to

bite but not every flash of white means
death. now i am grown and she is just a

devoted pussycat, learning to be more
careful with her grin.

tuesday, january 31

drive-thru at 9:30pm

& i'm screaming my lungs out
to kpop
    i don't understand the words
    i don't have to, you see

in my emerald green fluffy jacket
with my shiny gel nails
i'm bouncing in my seat
waiting for my turn at the mcdonald's drive-thru

& suddenly
        for the first time
            in a long time
                no, in my entire life!

i'm overcome with a sensation of being where i'm meant to be

i always suspected it would happen at a mcdonald's

i used to wonder if there's a universe
where everything works out
i think it might be this one

ACKNOWLEDGEMENTS

this is a poem about a bird originally appeared in the lady's slipper, issue 1.

maybe she's born with it, maybe it's trauma! originally appeared in the zinester's digest.

ABOUT THE AUTHOR

cait thomson (she/they) is a queer mama from ottawa, canada (unceded algonquin anishinabe land). cait writes about her experiences with mental illness, trauma recovery, and the natural world. her first chapbook *we need another word for this love* was published by bottlecap press in 2022. her poetry has appeared in a variety of canadian and international zines, anthologies, and online magazines. find cait on instagram @*thatlittlebeast*

ABOUT BEYOND THE VEIL PRESS

Beyond The Veil Press is a queer-owned indie publisher based in Colorado.

We began as a Kickstarter project by two SCAD graduates (Sarah Herrin & Josiah Callaway) in March 2021, with a goal to promote the healing power of poetry & art while lifting the veil from "scary" topics of mental health.

Since then, our small team of volunteers has grown to include AJ Wojtalik, Tyler Hurula, Kris Kaila, Salem Paige. (Visit our site to meet them!) We believe that by sharing our darkest stories, we find we are not alone.

We donate 10% of each anthology sale to a featured mental health nonprofit. Please see our mental health resources page on our website and on the following page.

beyondtheveilpress.com
IG: @beyondtheveilpress
FB: /beyondtheveilpress
Twt: @MrBiteyBTVPress

OTHER TITLES BY BEYOND THE VEIL PRESS

2023 - Coming soon!

Anthology 5
LGBTQ+ Pride Anthology
Chapbook Contest Series featuring: Marissa Forbes, Jess Cato, Teddy Goetz, Ashley Mezzano, & Kyrsta Morehouse.
Anthology 7
Neurotica For The Modern Doomscroller by Eddie Brophy

2023

We Apologize For The Inconvenience - Queer & Trans Voices (Club Q benefit issue)

2022

Anthology 2: Tea With My Monster
Heretic: A Story of Spiritual Liberation in Poems by Kristy Webster
Anti/Muse Adult Coloring Book
Anti/Muse Lined Notebooks
Anthology 3: How To Heal A Bloodline

2021

Anthology 1: There Is A Monster Inside That I Am Learning To Love
Anti/Muse: Poems by Sarah Herrin & Illustrations by Josiah Callaway

All books are (or will be) available in paperback and ebooks.

MENTAL HEALTH RESOURCES *we love*

Disclaimer: We are artists - not medical professionals. These recommendations are personal favorites and may not work for everyone. Please seek professional help if you are in crisis.

DIAL 988 IN A CRISIS

BOOKS

Permission to come home: reclaiming mental health as Asian Americans - Jenny Wang
The Pain We Carry: Healing from C-PTSD for People of Color - Natalie Gutierrez
Journey Through Trauma: A Trail Guide to the 5-Phase Cycle of Healing Repeated Trauma - Gretchen Schmelzer
The Deepest Well - Dr. Nadine Burke Harris
My Grandmother's Hands - Resmaa Menakem **tw: police violence*
What My Bones Know - Stephanie Foo (memoir)
The Journey From Abandonment To Healing – Susan Anderson
Waking The Tiger - Peter Levine
Polysecure: Attachment, Trauma, & Consensual Nonmonogamy – Jessica Fern
Self-Therapy: A Step-By-Step Guide to Healing Your Inner Child Using IFS - Jay Early
The Body Keeps The Score – Bessel van der Kolk **problematic but worth reading*

WEBSITES

activeminds.org - Mental health awareness and education for students.
afsp.org - Saving lives and bringing hope to those affected by suicide.
adaa.org - Anxiety & Depression Society of America
thetrevorproject.org - Crisis intervention and suicide prevention services for LGBTQ+ youth.
RAINN.org - for survivors of sexual assault

PODCASTS

Where Is My Mind? – Niall Breslin
The Hilarious World of Depression; Depreche Mode – John Moe
The Happiness Lab – Dr. Laurie Santos
Speaking of Psychology – Kim I. Mills
Being Well – Dr. Rick Hanson and Forrest Hanson

THANK YOU FOR SUPPORTING SMALL BUSINESS!

Made in the USA
Middletown, DE
03 December 2024